Counselling Skills

a quick guide

GW00725937

Cherry Eales and Chrissie Hawkes-Whitehead

DANIELS
AN IMPRINT OF FOLENS

Series Advisers

Gerald Haigh   Writer and Consultant in Education

Pauline Maskell   Secondary Head of Health Studies

John Sutton   General Secretary, Secondary Heads Association

Advisory Panel

Ruth Joyce   Adviser on Drugs and Health Education

Mike Kirby   Writer on Education

Terry Saunders   Secondary Head of Biology

Anne Morgan   Primary Deputy Headteacher

Elaine Wilson   Secondary Head of Science

ISBN: 1 85467 302 5

© Printed 1995, 1996

Folens Publishers
Albert House
Apex Business Centre
Boscombe Road
Dunstable LU5 4RL
Tel: 01582 472788   Fax: 01582 472575

Foreword

I like the idea of Quick Guides. Teachers need reliable information and advice on a very wide range of subjects related to their work and they need it to be accessible and concise. This series attempts to meet those needs by drawing on the knowledge of experienced practitioners and presenting the essential material in a format which facilitates rapid reference and provides valuable action checklists.

I am sure that these guides will be useful to teachers, to governors, to parents and indeed to all who are concerned with the effective management of all aspects of education.

John Sutton
General Secretary
Secondary Heads Association

About the author

Cherry Eales is a qualified teacher and counsellor with wide experience of training in all aspects of personal development.

Chrissie Hawkes-Whitehead is a freelance trainer, writer and consultant specialising in pastoral and professional development.

Contents

Counselling Skills: a quick guide

Introduction

This Quick Guide aims to outline the principles and practice of counselling and its application to many different situations. We want to point out early on that the skills of counselling are not necessarily the prerogative of trained counsellors. In fact a lot of the skills are ones we use on a daily basis with friends, colleagues, family and anyone who needs to work through something that is unclear or troubling them in some way.

This is not to say that there is not a role for trained, experienced counsellors who can help us to deal with difficult and complex issues. We need to have a clear idea of the boundaries of our responsibilities in using counselling skills in our everyday work and lives.

This is particularly true in education, where the scope of what we help students and colleagues deal with can extend far beyond what our job or role would ordinarily require. For instance, a student's work may be under par and, in the process of finding out why, we may discover that their girlfriend is pregnant, a friend is using drugs, Dad has just left home, or any one of a thousand and one other life crises may have arisen.

Referring people elsewhere

If the issue is too complex for you to help with, referring people on is often a dilemma. There may not be many options, particularly in rural areas or where funding for counselling projects and support services has been cut or was non-existent anyway.

If you do find yourself taking on a counselling role, make sure that you are aware of at least some of the avenues for referral at your disposal. Talk with colleagues and get information from libraries and local government agencies about appropriate services for young people in your area. Include in that information youth clubs and other programmes for young people; they will often have workers who can help young people with the difficulties and transitions they are going through.

Who counsels in schools?

It is not only teachers or designated school counsellors who take on a counselling role in educational establishments. School nurses, parents, students themselves and outside volunteers can also find themselves in counselling situations at any time. It is therefore important to ensure, as far as possible, that support and training are offered to help people to recognise and develop their skills and abilities in this area. They should also be aware of any school policy that affects counselling activities.

Where do I stand legally?

In any counselling-type interaction, confidentiality will be an issue. In a school, professional guidelines, and sometimes the law, require that certain types of abuse and criminal activity be reported if they comes to the attention of teaching or support staff.

This poses considerable problems in creating a climate of trust and safety where young people can talk freely and openly. It needs to be made clear from the outset that there are restrictions to confidentiality, and the young person may need to be referred to other people who, for this reason, may be able to help more effectively than you can.

What does counselling involve?

Helping people take responsibility for themselves, their decisions and their actions is one of the major tasks facing any teacher and counsellor. This is just as true for informal everyday counselling with a small 'c' as it is for the professional counsellor.

We hope that this Quick Guide will help you to gain an insight into what the counselling process is about and the skills necessary to do it effectively. By its very nature, the Guide does not give all the answers. Counselling on a professional level needs a lot of training to reach a point where the counsellor can cope with almost any situation.

Having said that, we are all natural counsellors in our everyday lives and have the necessary skills and abilities to some degree. Similarly, we all need support, reassurance that we are doing the best we can with what we have, and opportunities to learn and develop our skills.

We hope the Guide will clarify the counselling process for you and will encourage you and your organisation to develop policies, training and support to validate and enhance the skills and expertise available to young people and the people who work with them.

Aims of this Guide

This Quick Guide is designed to:

- give a working definition of counselling and explore its applications in school.
- consider what the Department of Education expects the role and responsibilities of teachers to be with regard to counselling.
- provide an overview of counselling process.
- explore the process of counselling and the relevant skills that would be useful to teachers and other staff in enhancing everyday communication with both colleagues and students.
- give insights into how to develop and integrate the principles of counselling into overall school policy.

A working definition of counselling

'Counselling should be seen not as a frill or an optional extra for those schools fortunate enough to be able to afford a counsellor but as a central and integral part of the educational process for all students.'

Newsome, Thorne and Wyld, *Student Counselling in Practice.*

There are many definitions of counselling. A useful exercise is to explore perceptions of what the word means in a particular context. The authors worked with a group of school teachers on 'counselling in the school environment' and came up with this definition:

'Counselling is building a trusting relationship and providing a safe space to allow people to explore their behaviour and emotions so that they can grow in self-awareness [and] self love and therefore increase their ability to relate to others.'

Bottisham Village College, Cambridgeshire, 1993.

Counselling as defined here relates to personal development. In teaching, we are always striving to ensure that we offer a balance of opportunity to develop both the person and his or her academic abilities.

'The basic requirements of an effective teaching relationship and an effective counselling relationship are one and the same, respect for each other, acceptance, trust, empathy, genuineness, non-possessive warmth, and congruence.'

Anne Jones, *Counselling Adolescents: School and After.*

Counselling is essentially a way of enabling people to help themselves.

Good communication skills are at the heart of both the counselling process and the teaching process.

Teaching does not just involve enabling students to learn about particular subjects and pass exams. The process of teaching also requires:

☐ classroom management skills

☐ support for students and colleagues

☐ motivational skills

☐ creation of a supportive school environment

Being successful in all of the above often comes down to having really good communication skills, and these are at the heart of the counselling process. A report by the Department for Education on *Discipline in Schools* (1989) says:

'We are convinced that there are skills, which all teachers need, involved in listening to young people and encouraging them to talk about their hopes and concerns before coming to a judgement about their behaviour. We consider that these basic counselling skills are particularly valuable… we therefore recommend that initial teacher training establishments should introduce all their students to basic counselling skills and their value… and we recommend that LEAs should provide in-service training in basic counselling skills for senior pastoral staff at least…'

Applications of counselling in school

Young people may come to school with a variety of problems and concerns, which could potentially become blocks to learning. Some of these might be:

- academic pressure
- a new relationship beginning
- physical or sexual abuse
- peer pressure
- a relationship ending
- friendship problems
- family break-up or divorce
- learning difficulties
- low self-esteem or poor self-image
- lack of confidence
- loss or bereavement
- bullying
- pregnancy

Considering the range of issues young people and adults may face in both education and their daily lives, it is not surprising that counselling support is needed.

Teachers need to recognise and acknowledge these and be equipped to respond effectively and appropriately. Remember that colleagues may also be experiencing some of the above events and may need counselling support of some kind. How far you decide to explore any of the above issues will inevitably be determined by time, your role and responsibilities, personal skills and how appropriate it is to your relationship with the other person.

A simple framework helps to clarify the counselling process.

In order to understand the counselling process, whether it be short- or long-term, a simple framework is helpful. The stages you might expect to go through could include:

1. Establishing an empathic relationship

At the beginning of the counselling relationship it is important to build up mutual trust and respect. This helps to create a supportive environment, to enable the student to feel heard and understood. The process begins even before any words have been spoken. For instance, the room you choose will play a part, as will the seating arrangements, the way you greet the person and your non-verbal communication. During the first phase the person is encouraged to share the issues and concerns that may be troubling him or her.

☐ For example:

Teacher: Jane, you seemed very upset during class today; would you like to tell me what is troubling you?

Jane: My younger brother is very ill in hospital and Mum has to spend all day with him. Everyone was so upset at home this morning and no one would help with the dishes and then Mr Jones screamed at me for not handing in my homework.

This first phase consists mainly of information gathering. In the above example, three linked issues become apparent. It is important to see the multiplicity of issues that people may be dealing with when they come to you in a stressed state. In this example, Jane is dealing with her own feelings about her brother being ill, everyone else being upset at home, extra housework for her and a teacher who is probably not aware of the home situation.

People come to counselling with a wide range of issues underlying the concern they originally presented.

2. Exploration of the present picture

At this stage the teacher is beginning to explore and assess Jane's beliefs, feelings, motives and goals.

Teacher: Jane, have you had a chance to see your brother in hospital? How do you feel about that? It sounds like you have to do a lot of the housework at the moment; how are you coping with that?

3. Establishing the desired outcome

The third stage involves the teacher helping Jane to identify how she would like the future to be and what needs to change for that to happen.

Teacher: Jane, you are going to be tied up at home for quite some time helping out. What do you need to help you cope better at school? How can you get what you need?

Counselling is not about taking over people's lives, but helping them take responsibility for sorting out their own problems.

4. Action

This stage involves working with the person to consider alternative attitudes, beliefs and actions, and encouraging a commitment to change.

☐ For instance:
Teacher: Jane, you say you have not been eating properly for some time, and you feel this may be linked to having no energy these days. Could we agree that you will eat some breakfast every morning and let me know how that is going next time we meet?

Focusing on something personal to Jane at this point is important, because it will probably be the only thing she is able to do something about herself. Getting people to focus on something they are in control of, and achieving something that will benefit them, will help them to begin to get other things in perspective.

Throughout the counselling process, it is important to encourage people to take responsibility for solving their own difficulties. Approaches like the one outlined above convey respect, trust and belief in the individual and their own ability to find ways of dealing with things in their lives which cause them concern.

Progression through these steps should ideally take place over a substantial period of time. There may be a number of sessions or meetings with the person where you would work through the stages with time to think and evaluate at each stage. This in itself can be helpful in enabling them to deal effectively with the issues that concern them. Alternatively, and this is much more likely in a school situation, you may have to compress the process into a short time frame.

Whether you have the chance to develop a proper counselling relationship, or have to deal with situations as they happen, this framework will help you focus your time effectively.

☐ For instance:
You may meet a person in the corridor who is obviously upset. You take them into a less public area, encourage them to share why they are upset and then help them to look at things from a different perspective and consider alternative ways of handling the situation.

An overview of the counselling process: the Step model:

4. Action

3. Establishing the desired outcome

2. Exploration of the present picture

1. Establishing an empathic relationship

Empathy and establishing rapport

It is important to establish rapport and develop an empathic relationship early on in the counselling process.

An effective counselling process depends upon establishing good rapport and developing an empathic relationship. This will allow issues to be discussed freely and safely. It is important to spend time on this at the beginning of any type of counselling process, even if the time you have is limited. You will find that both of you will get a lot more out of however much time you have.

So, what is rapport and how does it contribute to developing an empathic relationship? Rapport is the feeling of connection with people we get when we feel that we are on their wavelength and that we are accepted and acknowledged as ourselves. In order to achieve this, we need to be able to assure each other that we will be heard and that we have a basic respect for each other. This does not mean we have to agree with people or condone everything they think, feel or do; we just need to acknowledge that the way they see things is different and perhaps no less valid. The way to start to establish rapport is to:

- [ ] let the person know you have some time for them.
- [ ] find as comfortable a place as possible to talk.
- [ ] talk about mundane things for a minute, the weather or something, just to give you both breathing space before beginning.
- [ ] adopt similar 'body language' to the other person, so that they feel comfortable with you: gestures, the way you sit or stand and so on. Sit or stand close enough for you both to be comfortable, but not too close.

Counselling Skills: a quick guide

Empathy and establishing rapport
(continued)

Above all, you must want to be with the person; if you don't, this will quickly come across and make any effort at establishing rapport difficult. Once you have established some rapport and have begun to talk the issue through, you need to build and maintain it by:

An empathic relationship needs a non-threatening, accepting atmosphere in which to develop.

- establishing and maintaining good eye contact.
- smiling and nodding as appropriate.
- using reassuring gestures and touch as appropriate.
- continuing to 'mirror' body language as inconspicuously as possible.

If all the above are in place, you will feel an empathic relationship developing. An empathic relationship depends upon the counsellor creating a non-threatening, accepting atmosphere in which the other person feels heard and understood. It also depends a lot on your willingness to put yourself in their shoes, so that you can acknowledge the situation and help them to find a way of dealing with it.

One important distinction we need to make here is between empathy and sympathy. When you sympathise with someone you acknowledge the situation and share their feelings. With empathy, you are developing a deeper rapport or connection, to enable you to help the person work through a problem in a way that will alleviate its effects.

Counselling skills can help in building relationships which motivate and encourage people to grow and learn.

The ability to develop empathic relationships and establish and maintain rapport requires a number of basic communication skills that we all have at our fingertips. Many of us already have intuitive communication skills, which we may use in our work. We can, however, use these more effectively if we complement our intuition with developed counselling skills.

We are all good communicators and as teachers, or other staff working with and alongside young people, we have probably developed these skills to a greater degree than we might otherwise have done.

Counselling in any shape or form requires us to pay particular attention to some key communication skills. We need to be continually aware of our ability to implement these skills in the wide variety of counselling-type situations we might find ourselves in.

The next section of this guide will outline some key skills in some detail in order to clarify their importance in counselling. The ones we have chosen to focus on are:

- effective listening skills
- 'reflecting'
- recognising non-verbal cues
- questioning and prompting

1. Effective listening skills

The skill of really listening is the most fundamental counselling skill of all. Listening intently involves total concentration. Some key points to remember when listening to people are:

Listening effectively sounds easy, but it requires the total concentration of all the listener's faculties.

- Attend with your ears to what the person is saying.
- Attend with your eyes to their body language.
- Attend to your own reactions and feelings to what is being said.

It is important to be aware of all these in order to get a complete picture of what is going on.

Key rules for effective listening

- Focusing:
  - The person speaking has the listener's undivided attention.
  - The listener maintains eye contact at a comfortable and appropriate level, not staring continually.
- Giving non-verbal encouragement:
  - Nods, smiles and expressions of understanding from the listener help communicate acceptance, respect and interest; this allows the person to feel comfortable about exploring thoughts and sharing experiences
  - Accepting silences, allowing the person time to reflect and work out what they want to say, is also important.
- Do not judge the other person:
  - It is important that the listener tries to understand the world through the other person's eyes. A difficulty we frequently face in counselling is that we get caught up in our own views, feelings and attitudes to the presenting problem and think that we have all the answers.

The world is full of possible distractions, but effective listening skills will help us keep them in their place.

Barriers to effective listening

With the best will in the world, the listener's attention may not be entirely free and available to the person speaking. There may be a variety of reasons for this. Some of these might be:

☐ internal distractions
- tiredness
- hunger
- feeling burdened by our own problems
- daydreaming
- anxiety
- needing to be somewhere else
- personal dislike or fear of the person
- prejudice against the person's viewpoint

☐ external distractions
- noise
- lack of privacy

The last two barriers highlight the difficulties we encounter in trying to listen in a totally unbiased way to students or colleagues. Our own values, attitudes and experiences can distort the process. However, the more we develop the skills of effective listening, the less likely we are to be sidetracked by our own thoughts and ideas.

2. Reflecting

This does not mean reflecting in the sense of thinking about something, but showing someone what they have communicated, in the same way that a mirror shows us what we look like.

The skill of reflecting involves the person in the counselling role clarifying what the issues are by:

- gaining an understanding of what the person is concerned about and the feelings associated with those concerns.
- reflecting both the factual content and the feelings back to the other person, to enable them to hear their concerns out loud and begin the process of dealing with them. It also enables you to check whether what they have said is what they really mean.

Remember that you may not reflect feelings or facts accurately the first time, so allow time for clarification.

As we have said, there are two types of reflective response. These are:

- the reflection of content
- the reflection of feelings

We will now go on to look at each of these ways of responding in more depth.

Separating the factual content from the person's feelings allows greater clarity.

Reflecting content

The literal meaning of a person's words is mirrored by restating them in a slightly different form, separating out the feeling and the factual content.

☐ For example:
Susan is tearful and fidgety, looking down most of the time and clenching her fists every now and then. Her breathing is erratic and she is sighing a lot. With her arms folded, she eventually says, very quickly, in a high, erratic voice, 'I am furious with my mother, she doesn't care about me and what I want, she is going to leave Dad and I have to go with her so I will have to leave this school and all my friends here.'

☐ In this example, reflecting back the content would include:
'Your mother seems to have made a decision to separate from your father and take responsibility for you. As a result of the separation you may have to move elsewhere.'

Separating the factual content from the feelings the person is expressing, and paraphrasing this back to them, enables both of you to begin to focus more clearly on how the issues can be dealt with effectively. This is exaggerated here to make the point; in practice you would move from content to feeling or *vice versa* much more fluidly.

Reflect back feelings

'Susan, it sounds as if you feel angry and hurt that your mother has not asked you how you feel about what the separation might mean for you, and you feel she does not care either.'

In the process of counselling, people will use 'feeling' words. For instance, Susan uses the word 'furious'. The role of the counsellor is to reflect back, as accurately as possible, the meaning behind the words they have used. For example, 'furious' means much the same as 'angry'. Reflecting back a slightly different word enables the person to widen their exploration of their feelings.

The skill of reflective responding helps the counsellor to build up effective rapport. The person will feel they have been understood and helped to clarify the situation and how they feel about it.

Reflective responding allows a progression towards an accurate understanding of the person's situation and how they feel about it.

Communication is only effective if either:

☐ the communicators match what they say verbally and how they express it physically.

or

☐ any mismatches are recognised and acknowledged as part of the interaction.

Non-verbal signals may or may not match what is being said. Watch out for incongruities.

The face and body are extremely communicative. It is therefore very important to 'listen' to and learn to recognise the messages given out physically and whether these messages match what is being said verbally. For instance:

☐ **Facial expressions:** smiles, frowns, raised eyebrows, twisted lips.

☐ **Posture:** standing or sitting straight or hunched, exaggerated body movements.

☐ **Gestures:** pointing, clenched fists.

☐ **Behaviour:** fidgeting, pacing up and down.

☐ **Physiology:** quickened breathing, blushing or paleness, perspiration.

☐ **Voice:** pitch, intensity, inflection, pauses, silences and fluency.

3. Recognising non-verbal cues
(continued)

All of the above will provide the first indications of what might be happening to the person. Far more may be conveyed about the situation through non-verbal cues than by the spoken word itself. In the example we used in the previous section, a lot of information was available to us about how Susan might be feeling from her:

Posture, gestures and physiological signs can tell us more about someone's feelings than what they say.

- **Posture:** Susan had her head down.
- **Gestures:** she kept clenching her fists.
- **Physiology:** her breathing was erratic and she kept sighing.

These elements of the interaction account for around 60% of initial communication and tone of voice accounts for about 33%. Susan's voice was high-pitched and erratic, which reinforces the other messages about how she is feeling.

With the information you have from the above scenario, you could begin to establish rapport easily by noticing Susan's erratic breathing and asking her to sit quietly for a moment and catch her breath, then gently encourage her to breathe a little more deeply. This in itself will help her to calm down and start to think about things a little more clearly.

Communication breakdown

When we first encounter someone, the initial communication consists approximately of:

- [ ] body language, such as gestures, as well as physiological signs such as breathing = 60%.
- [ ] tone of voice = 33%.
- [ ] Words = 7%.

4. Prompting and questioning

There are times in the counselling process when the skill of prompting and probing sensitively and appropriately is required. The person being counselled may talk in quite vague terms about their concerns and feelings. It is important to help them to describe the problem accurately, so that you can understand, as far as possible, the meaning of the emotional words they are using. The word 'upset' for example has a number of possible meanings.

Sensitive prompting and questioning help us work towards a deeper understanding of the situation.

To prompt effectively, you need to be able to ask questions that direct the person's attention towards clarifying the situation and exploring their feelings around it.

As well as the questions you ask, it is important to be aware of how you ask them. Your body language and voice need to remain non-judgemental and encouraging.

This type of question will enable the person to focus on the specific problem rather than looking at it in a more generalised way. This begins the process of getting things in perspective and moving away from seeing the problem as an all-encompassing one.

The judicious use of questions helps to keep the conversation focused on the relevant issues.

☐ Use prompt phrases to encourage dialogue, for example:
- 'Tell me more about...'
- 'I don't think I understand what you mean by...'
- 'Please go on...'

☐ Use non-verbal prompts like nodding and eye contact to show you understand and are interested.

☐ Use questions to keep the focus on the person. It is important to help the person remain focused on the relevant and important issues.

One way of doing this is to have the person ask relevant questions of themselves. For instance:

☐ **Counsellor**: John, if you had to ask yourself a question about this situation right now, what would it be?

☐ **John** (pausing a long time): It might be 'Why am I so afraid of Tom? He has not actually hurt me yet.'

In this example, the counsellor puts the ball in John's court, encouraging him to take responsibility for his part in looking for ways of dealing with the situation.

Some tips on prompting and questioning

☐ Ask open ended questions which encourage the
person to elaborate:

- What?
- How?
- Who?
- When?

☐ Pick up any generalisations the person might use,
for instance:

- 'People are always picking on me'

  Counsellor: 'Always?'

  'Which people?'

  'When does it happen?'

  'Who has picked on you lately?'

  'What sort of things do they say to
  you?'

- 'I hate her!'

  Counsellor: 'What has she done that makes
  you feel that?'

  'When did it start?'

  'If she were here now, what would
  you want to say to her?'

*Use open ended
questions to
encourage the
person to talk.
Counselling is not
interrogation.*

Counselling Skills: a quick guide

Don't bombard the person with questions. Learn to be comfortable with silence.

Tips on what not to do in prompting and questioning

☐ Do not use questions to fill up silence.
Learn to be comfortable with silences and if possible, after a reasonable interval, reflect back what the silence might mean. For instance:

- 'You have been very quiet for the last few minutes; were you thinking through what you said?'

☐ Avoid asking 'why' questions too much; they can make people feel they are being interrogated.

☐ Do not overdo questioning. Give people space to think things through. Too many questions may only confuse their thinking.

☐ Finally, remember that you are responding to the person and taking the lead from them, rather than leading the conversation yourself. Everything you say should be a response to something they have said.

Confidentiality

'Confidential': spoken or written in confidence, to be kept secret.

Concise Oxford Dictionary

One of the golden rules of counselling is to respect confidentiality; that is, whatever is said within the counselling process goes no further unless the person being counselled decides otherwise.

This poses considerable difficulty for the classroom teacher in defining how confidential the information discussed can remain. For instance, in cases of abuse you are under a legal obligation to disclose anything of an illegal nature that involves a child in your care. Teachers have a legal responsibility to report sexual and physical abuse and situations where there appears to be danger to others.

All you can do in situations of this kind is to make it clear from the beginning that there are some issues that require the involvement of outside help and expertise and that because of your position you cannot enable the person to deal with their situation without that help.

Always ensure that people are not left with nowhere to go because of this. If they do not want to discuss their problems with you because of the dilemma you face over confidentiality, refer them to a counselling service appropriate to their situation, which will be able to help them confidentially.

Confidentiality is the bedrock of counselling, but teachers have a legal responsibility to report certain circumstances to the authorities.

Contracting and setting boundaries

Establish the counselling 'contract' early in the relationship.

It is important at the beginning of any counselling relationship that all parties are clear, as far as possible, about what they can and cannot expect. It is advisable to contract the following with the person being counselled:

☐ the time you and they are able to allocate. For instance, 'We have half an hour to talk this through, so we will finish by 3 pm.'

☐ where the counselling takes place. If there will be more than one session, try to ensure as far as possible that they are in the same place at a regular time.

☐ boundaries of confidentiality: what can be disclosed to others and what cannot.

☐ to ensure there are no interruptions and the environment, as far as possible, allows you to create a safe space for the person to explore the issues that concern them.

☐ to be clear about whether you are the most appropriate person to discuss these issue or concerns with.

☐ to advise the person where to go for further support and information if it is required. If someone needs long-term counselling in depth, they will need to be referred elsewhere.

Incorporating counselling skills into school life

Having talked throughout this Guide about the process of counselling and the skills needed to undertake it effectively, we need to explore ways that the school environment can support counselling as a valid and necessary part of education.

A group of teachers from the Cambridgeshire area came up with the following areas in which counselling could be incorporated:

- **Initial teacher training:** adequate training in communication skills and basic techniques of counselling should be part of the curriculum of any teacher training course.
- **In-service training:** opportunities to review current counselling processes and their relevance to education should be made available as part of in service training, as should opportunities for all teachers to learn and review the skills and techniques of counselling.

If counselling initiatives of any kind are to succeed, a supportive environment must be developed, in which:

- teachers are willing and able to listen to students or other staff members.
- the physical environment is comfortable and friendly.
- the development of peer support initiatives for both colleagues and students is encouraged. (These can be incorporated in existing structures such as tutor groups and mentoring programmes.)
- there are trained counsellors in each year group.
- parents and governors can obtain training in counselling skills.

Individual counselling can only be fully effective if the school ethos encourages listening, empathy and support for its members.

Clear guidelines and information on counselling should be part of the school's policy.

The Cambridgeshire group came up with the following list of things that would need to be taken into account when incorporating counselling into school policy documents.

- Guidelines on counselling and what it means for the individual school.

- The roles and responsibilities of staff in relation to counselling and similar support for colleagues and students.

- The legal requirements of teachers in situations where young people disclose sexual or physical abuse or anything else of an illegal nature.

- Advice on what to do if staff are unsure about their role.

- Training requirements of staff in relation to counselling skills.

- Existing and future training opportunities.

Conclusion

This Quick Guide has tried to cover as comprehensively as possible the basic elements of the counselling process. It has outlined ideas and information that may be helpful to you in the counselling you may already be doing as part of the everyday educational experience.

We also hope it will enable you to encourage the development of policy guidelines and strategies to help the counselling process to be better recognised, valued and supported in the school or college as a whole.

Professional support and training are available for anyone involved with counselling, and can be invaluable.

Training and support are important prerequisites for anyone undertaking a counselling role of any kind. We would recommend that both initial and in-service training should include theoretical and practical, skill-based elements of counselling. Adult education programmes often include counselling courses and could provide outside training opportunities and facilitators and speakers on the subject.

The British Association of Counselling offers associate membership to people who have little or no formal training or qualification in counselling but nonetheless find themselves doing it as part of their everyday work. Membership gives you a code of ethics, access to insurance policies specific to the field and a professional journal, as well as advice and support.

Adlerian Society of Great Britain
Cathy Parsons
Administrator
77 Clissold Crescent
London N16 9AR
telephone 0171-923 2472

Anti-Bullying Campaign
10 Borough High Street
London SE1 9QQ
helpline 0171-378 8374 (will help schools
set up anti-bullying policies)

British Association for Counselling (BAC)
1 Regent Place
Rugby
Warwickshire CV21 2PJ
telephone 01788 550899
information line 01788 578328 (recording)

Childline
2nd floor, Royal Mail Building
Studd Street
London N1 0QW
telephone 0171-239 1000
helpline 0800 1111

The Children's Legal Centre Ltd.
20 Compton Terrace
London N1 2UN
helpline 0171-359 6251 (2–5 pm Monday
to Friday)

Youth Access
Magazine Business Centre
11 Newarke Street
Leicester LE1 5SS
telephone 0116 255 8763
(National Association of Young People's
Counselling and Advisory Services)

Bibliography

Nigel Collins, *On the Spot: a guidance and counselling handbook*, Oxford University Press 1985.

Discipline in Schools: report of the Committee of Enquiry Chaired by Lord Elton, (Department of Education and Science) HMSO 1989.

Gerard Egan, *The Skilled Helper*, 4th edition, Brooks Cole 1990.

Gerard Egan, *You and Me: the Skills of Communicating and Relating to Others*, Brooks Cole 1977.

Sean Haldane, *Emotional First Aid: A Crisis Handbook*, Crucible 1990.

Linda Hill, D*eveloping Counselling Skills in Work with Adolescents*, National Council of Voluntary Child Care Organisations 1987.

Michael Jacobs, *Still Small Voice: An Introduction to Counselling in Pastoral and Other Settings*, New Library of Pastoral Care, SPCK 1993.

Anne Jones, *Counselling Adolescents: School and After*, 2nd edition, Kogan Page 1984.

Eugene Kennedy, *Crisis Counselling: The Essential Guide for Non-professional Counsellors*, Gill & Macmillan 1981.

R Martin, *Teaching Through Encouragement*, Prentice Hall 1980.

Anthea Millar, *Counselling Skills, Set A: An Introduction*, Folens Ltd 1996. (First published in 1989 by Daniels Publishing)

Anthea Millar, *Counselling Skills, Set B: Counselling and Co-operation in the Classroom*, Folens Ltd 1996. (First published in 1991 by Daniels Publishing)

Audrey Newsome, Brian J Thorne and Keith L Wyld, *Student Counselling in Practice*, University of London Press 1973.

Ellen Noonan, *Counselling Young People*, Methuen 1983.

Bibliography (continued)

Carl Rogers, *Client Centered Therapy,* Constable 1965.

T D Vaughan, *Concepts of Counselling,* Bedford Square Press 1975.

Tom Wylie, *One Way of Helping: A Practical Guide to Counselling Young People Informally,* Youth Work Press 1993.

Developing Assertiveness Skills 2nd edition
Chrissie Hawkes-Whitehead
ISBN 1 85467 212 6

The Assertiveness Game
Eliot Franks
ISBN 1 85467 183 9

Power in the Workplace
Maureen LaJoy
ISBN 1 85467 193 6

Body Language
Ursula Markham
ISBN 85467 165 0

Countering Sexual Harassment
Dr Carrie M H Herbert
ISBN 1 85467 213 4

Active Listening: A Counselling Skills Approach
Anthea Millar and Angela Cameron
ISBN 1 85467 186 3

Developing Peer Counselling Skills
Maggie Phillips and Joan Sturkie
ISBN 1 85467 189 8

Using Peer Counselling Skills
Maggie Phillips and Joan Sturkie
ISBN 1 85467 190 1

Raising Self Esteem: 50 Activities
Murray White
ISBN 1 85467 231 1

Self Esteem: Its Meaning and Value in Schools A and B
Murray White
ISBNs 1 85467 141 3 and 1 85467 142 1

Folens resource packs are:

✓ *Fully photocopiable*

✓ *Ready for use*

✓ *Flexible*

✓ *Clearly designed*

✓ *Tried and tested*

✓ *Cost-effective*

The Quick Guide series from Folens

Quick Guides are up to date, stimulating and readable A5 booklets, packed with essential information and key facts on important issues in education.

Health education

Drugs Education for children aged 4–11: A Quick Guide
Janice Slough
ISBN 1 85467 326 2

Drugs Education for children aged 11–18: A Quick Guide
Janice Slough
ISBN 1 85467 324 6

Alcohol: A Quick Guide
Dr Gerald Beales
ISBN 1 85467 300 9

Smoking Issues: A Quick Guide
Paul Hooper
ISBN 1 85467 309 2

Sex Education: A Quick Guide for Teachers
Dr Michael Kirby
ISBN 1 85467 228 2

Sex Education for children aged 4–11: A Quick Guide for parents and carers
Janice Slough
ISBN 1 85467 312 2

Sex Education for children aged 11–18: A Quick Guide for parents and carers
Janice Slough
ISBN 1 85467 313 0

Career enhancement

Assertiveness: A Quick Guide
Chrissie Hawkes-Whitehead
ISBN 1 85467 305 X

Counselling: A Quick Guide
Chrissie Hawkes-Whitehead
and Cherry Eales
ISBN 1 85467 302 5

Problem People and How to Handle Them: A Quick Guide
Ursula Markham
ISBN 1 85467 317 3

Class and school management

Bullying: A Quick Guide
Dr Carrie Herbert
ISBN 1 85467 323 8

School Inspections: A Quick Guide
Malcolm Massey
ISBN 1 85467 308 4

Grief, Loss and Bereavement: A Quick Guide
Penny Casdagli & Francis Gobey
ISBN 1 85467 307 6

Safety on Educational Visits: A Quick Guide
Michael Evans
ISBN 1 85467 306 8

Equal Opportunities: A Quick Guide
Gwyneth Hughes & Wendy Smith
ISBN 1 85467 303 3

Working in Groups: A Quick Guide
Pauline Maskell
ISBN 1 85467 304 1

Organising Conferences and Events: A Quick Guide
David Napier
ISBN 1 85467 314 9

Working with Parents: A Quick Guide
Dr Michael Kirby
ISBN 1 85467 315 7

For further information

For further details of any of our publications mentioned in this Quick Guide, please fill in and post this form (or a photocopy) to:

Folens Publishers   Tel: 01582 472788

Albert House   Fax: 01582 472575

Apex Business Centre

Boscombe Road

Dunstable LU5 4RL

Name ....

Job Title ....

Organisation ....

Address ....

....

Postcode ....

Tel No. ....

Fax No. ....

☐   **Please send me details of the following publications:**

Notes

Counselling Skills: a quick guide

Notes

Notes

Counselling Skills: a quick guide

Notes

Notes

Counselling Skills: a quick guide